Let's Have an Adventure

Playground

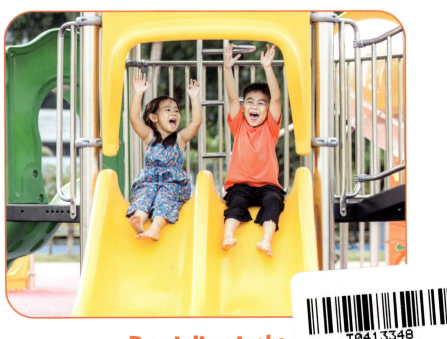

By Julia Jaske

2 I see swings on the playground.

I see slides on the playground.

4 I see tunnels on the playground.

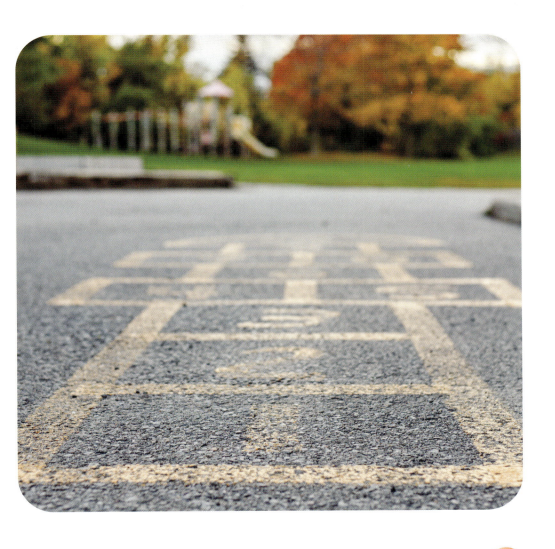

I see hopscotch on the playground.

I see seesaws on the playground.

I see sand on the playground.

8. I see games on the playground.

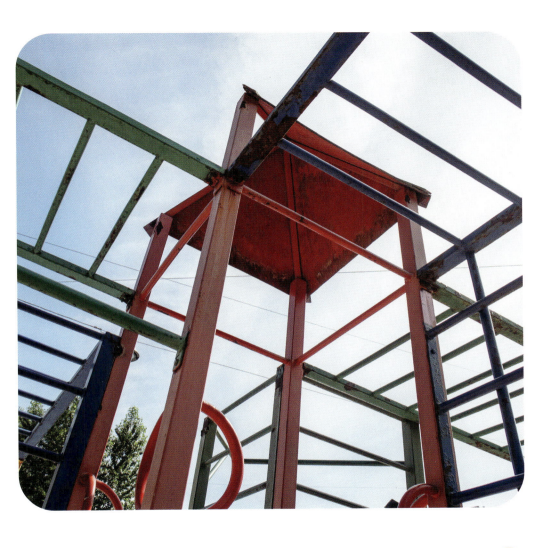

I see bars on the playground.

I see chalk on the playground.

I see bridges on the playground.

12 I see climbers on the playground.

I see rings on the playground.

Word List

playground	games
swings	bars
slides	chalk
tunnels	bridges
hopscotch	climbers
seesaws	rings
sand	

72 Words

I see swings on the playground.
I see slides on the playground.
I see tunnels on the playground.
I see hopscotch on the playground.
I see seesaws on the playground.
I see sand on the playground.
I see games on the playground.
I see bars on the playground.
I see chalk on the playground.
I see bridges on the playground.
I see climbers on the playground.
I see rings on the playground.

Published in the United States of America by Cherry Lake Publishing Group
Ann Arbor, Michigan
www.cherrylakepublishing.com

Book Designer: Melinda Millward

Photo Credits: Cover: © Robert Kneschke/Shutterstock; page 1: © Sorapop Udomsri/Shutterstock; page 2: © Aime Holzbach/Shutterstock; page 3: © Joeprachatree/Shutterstock; page 4: © mantinov/Shutterstock; page 5: © Iryna Tolmachova/Shutterstock; page 6: © Stor24/Shutterstock; page 7: © Oleksii Synelnykov/Shutterstock; page 8: © Maria Shipakina/Shutterstock; page 9: © Akintevs/Shutterstock; page 10: © Jurgis Mankauskas/Shutterstock; page 11: © MJTH/Shutterstock; page 12: © Satheesh Cholakkal/Shutterstock; page 13: © ANDY RELY/Shutterstock; page 14: © Antonova Ganna/Shutterstock

Copyright © 2023 by Cherry Lake Publishing Group
All rights reserved. No part of this book may be reproduced or utilized in any form or by any means without written permission from the publisher.

Cherry Blossom Press is an imprint of Cherry Lake Publishing Group.

Library of Congress Cataloging-in-Publication Data

Names: Jaske, Julia, author.
Title: Playground / written by Julia Jaske.
Description: Ann Arbor, Michigan : Cherry Lake Publishing, [2023] | Series: Let's have an adventure | Audience: Grades 2-3. | Summary: "Time for an adventure! Meet us at the playground! Do you know what you'll see while you're there? Books in the Let's Have an Adventure series use the Whole Language approach to literacy, combining sight words and repetition to build recognition and confidence. Keeping the text simple makes reading through these books easy and fun. Bold, colorful photographs that align directly with the text help readers with comprehension throughout the book"—Provided by publisher.
Identifiers: LCCN 2022038084 | ISBN 9781668919088 (paperback) | ISBN 9781668922767 (pdf) | ISBN 9781668921432 (ebook)
Subjects: LCSH: Playgrounds—Juvenile literature.
Classification: LCC GV423 .J37 2023 | DDC 796.06/8—dc23/eng/20220830
LC record available at https://lccn.loc.gov/2022038084

Cherry Lake Publishing Group would like to acknowledge the work of the Partnership for 21st Century Learning, a Network of Battelle for Kids. Please visit http://www.battelleforkids.org/networks/p21 for more information.

Printed in the United States of America
Corporate Graphics